# GEORG TRAKL: POEMS

# GEORG TRAKL
# POEMS

Translated by
Stephen Tapscott

**Oberlin College Press**
Oberlin, Ohio

The FIELD Translation Series, vol. 30
Oberlin College Press, 50 N. Professor Street, Oberlin, OH 44074
www.oberlin.edu/ocpress

Cover and book design: Steve Farkas.
Cover art: Georg Trakl, *Self-Portrait*, reproduced by kind permission of the
Georg Trakl Memorial and Research Center, Salzburg, Austria.

**Library of Congress Cataloging-in-Publication Data**

Trakl, Georg, 1887–1914.
[Poems. English. Selections]
Georg Trakl : poems / translated by Stephen Tapscott.
    p. cm. — (The FIELD translation series ; v.30)
ISBN-13: 978-0-932440-42-6 (pbk. : alk. paper)
ISBN-10: 0-932440-42-8 (pbk. : alk. paper)
1. Trakl, Georg, 1887–1914—Translations into English.  I. Tapscott, Stephen, 1948–
    II. Title.
PT2642.R22A266 2011
831'.912—dc23
                                2011024539

# Contents

# Foreword

I think the time is right for a fresh translation of Georg Trakl's work. The poems are stunning, crisp and austerely elegant, breathless as cold vodka; his story haunts, especially at the centenary of World War I; and the relations between his life and his craft raise questions of a sort that each poetic generation needs to renegotiate on its own terms. These brisk rich harsh poems have a lot to teach us; they demanded a discipline of him, and they exact a strange disciplined pleasure from their readers, too, a kind of egoless Romanticism we have to silence ourselves in order to hear.

Trakl (1887–1914) was Austrian, raised in a prosperous bourgeois Protestant family in the center of Salzburg. The city is a fortress-and-festival town, its inner ring an arena of horses and fountains and Baroque horse-fountains: a conservative regime of Catholic-Habsburg elegance, ringed by sublime blue mountains. The landscape, the alienation even in the face of physical beauty, the intensity and purity of a childhood sense-of-place, the synesthesic colors — these components recur, eventually, as elements in the mythology of Trakl's adult poems. Implausibly, Trakl develops later into an attentive poet of place, even down to the arches of the beer-gardens and the marble tombstones and statues of his city. (Unlikely as it seems, the Mirabell Gardens in Salzburg now boast a plaque with Trakl's eerie poem about almost overhearing Mozart music there.) After the birth of six children, his mother retreated into depression and opium; the father, already austere, withdrew further; the surviving four children were raised by a French-speaking governess, apparently a woman of strong Catholicism and devout superstitions.

Sent to a classical lyceum, by the end of his seventh year there Trakl had failed Latin, Greek, and math. After repeating one year, he was allowed to end his "humanistic" education and to start to train as a chemical pharmacist. (His choice of career may have been influenced by the availability of recreational drugs in the field.) He spent several troubled and lonely years at the University of Vienna, then moved back to Salzburg. After his father's death in 1910, he began to travel, drifting — in desperation and often in poverty — : to Vienna, to Innsbruck, back to Salzburg. Drafted into the Austro-Hungarian army, he was posted to Innsbruck in 1912; he was already writing poems that sound like "Trakl," but he and his work were solitary and stalled, his quatrains repeating in what he later called a "merry-go-round" formal regularity, their tone a self-reflexive melancholy.

In Innsbruck the young poet was befriended by writers associated with Ludwig von Ficker and his influential new magazine *Der Brenner*, where Trakl's poems soon began to appear beside works by other writers associated with the new "Expressionism." From 1912 through the last years of Trakl's short life, Ficker sponsored and supported the difficult young man: he sustained Trakl through his drug and alcohol addictions, his hostilities and suspicions, his sometimes pathological shyness and social awkwardness. To support Trakl, Ficker arranged also for an anonymous stipend from their mutual friend in Vienna, Ludwig Wittgenstein. The works of Ficker and of other members of the Brenner circle offered Trakl liberating affirmations, in a sort of earnest Christian proto-Existentialism. Paradoxically, the prophetic future-orientation of Nietzsche opened for Trakl a path that looked backward, toward an idealized prelinguistic condition that Trakl associated with childhood, that "blue cave."

These influences helped Trakl in Innsbruck to move from the pastel melancholy of his earlier poems toward the unornamented "mirror-image-world" (in Rilke's phrase) of his middle-period work (from 1912 onward); the new method is not Rilke's confident address to a mysterious emergent self, but a summoning of the austere conditions for the production of that self. His repetitions in those middle and later poems, reworking the same images in new contexts, serve a ritual, cumulative function, in the creation of an internally consistent myth. Even the colors in the poems — crimson, blue, silver, black — repeat in a classic *Jugendstil* palette. With a tone of awe, Ficker writes to Trakl in 1913:

> Your... word[s] come from a depth that no longer belongs to you, a depth which has risen out of you, presented itself to me, and now belongs to me. It is a depth that cancels out and rises above the personal.

This illusion of impersonal depth is one of the strongest effects that Trakl's poems had on Rilke, I think: in the conviction that the poem does not arise from suffering and abjection, but that such experiences have an interiorizing effect, opening spaces for a self to inhabit. This effect accounts, too, for some of Trakl's uncanny landscape descriptions, in which the physical world presents itself as component energies in the mystery of which the observer is a part. The poem does not "express" the cryptic self nor read the physical world as an allegory, so much as it details dynamic facts of the physical world — seasons and landscapes and times of day — as if they were already constituent elements of the self. German critics have observed how, although they are sometimes described as "Expressionist," Trakl's grammar and perceptions approach the lucidity of mathematics.

Trakl found analogies for his new aspirations also in the works of Novalis and Hölderlin and Rimbaud and, clearly, Nietzsche. Although he is read as a psychological poet, Trakl seems not to have responded strongly to Freud. He did admire the stunned saintliness of some of Dostoevsky's characters, the satire of Karl Kraus, the intensity of Expressionist paintings.[1] In his own self-portrait (1913–14), the face is the color of chloro-

---

[1] In his poem "The Storm," for instance, Trakl seems to be embedding descriptions of Oskar Kokoschka's painting "Windsbraut" ("The Tempest," literally "The Bride of the Wind").

form, the crests of its features outlined in slabs of ocher. The spherical head sits on a shadowy collar as round as a plate. The eyes are open; the small mouth, dimly smiling, is clamped shut.

In the poems of his Innsbruck years, Trakl sometimes creates alter egos (Helian, Sebastian, Elis), who carry heavily the burden of selfhood; sometimes self-annulment seems to them like a blessed option (in silences, relinquishments, pauses, death), and sometimes the pressures of consciousness force their language into oblique or gnomic articulations. The complement to these figures is the Sister, an image of grace and transcendent presence who hovers above the battlefield of the soul, promising. Like the immanent spirituality of the material world, like the small blue flower (an image that Trakl adapts from Novalis), she is both possible and distant, hope and prohibition. The Sister may be a version of Trakl's own beloved sister Grete, whose unhappy marriage in Berlin precipitated a crisis in Trakl's emotional life. (Their letters remain controlled and unpublished.) I resist the slightly prurient attempt by biographical criticism to speculate about the nature of that sibling relation. I think it's clear that the poems' irrational hope for reunion with the figure of the Sister involves some kind of incestuous energy, but more importantly — as with many German and British Romantic writers — I think that that hope registers a Jungian gesture toward an internal integration as well, accompanied by a desire for the poem to move "beyond" language. The dynamic presupposes extraordinary attachment and loss, but it works toward visionary compensation. The Virgo (as in "The Heart," the first poem of Trakl's stunning final series) is the astrological sign of autumn; throughout Trakl's poems after 1914 and his return to the army, she appears also as the Nun, the soul's companion, the perfect Friend.

In the autumn of 1914, Trakl's commission in the Austrian army was renewed. He was posted to Southern Poland, assigned as a medic on the basis of his ramshackle training in pharmacology. In Galicia on the Eastern Front, after the bloody and chaotic battle of Grodek, in the absence of better-trained medical personnel Trakl found himself in charge of a field hospital of almost a hundred wounded soldiers. Without competence to treat them, lacking even adequate supplies, Trakl felt helpless. He found intolerable the facts of the human suffering — the physical squalor, the cries of the wounded. Within sight of the camp, the army command punished partisan peasants by hanging them, leaving their decaying bodies on display, as warnings, in the trees.

After three days, in desperation, Trakl shot himself in the head. He failed to kill himself. Moved to a garrison hospital in Krakow, he was diagnosed with *dementia praecox*, treated with opiates, and locked in a cell with a fellow patient who was dying of alcoholism. Notified of the emergency, Ficker hurriedly left Salzburg, and Wittgenstein set out from Vienna. They arrived too late. Under observation in Krakow, Trakl apparently hoarded medicines from his doctors; on November 3, 1914, he died of an overdose of cocaine. He was twenty-seven years old. His writing career had lasted, at most, six years. The poems he had written during this last period (beginning with "The Heart") form an accomplished, intense sequence that brings together many of the tropes, techniques, and metaphors that had seemed disparate, in earlier poems.

That autumn Wittgenstein began his second manuscript, published as the *Notebooks, 1914–16*, which began a set of questions that he would follow through to the full *Tractatus* (1918). In both texts he proposes the representational "logical form" of language, but his argument is haunted by a shadow-question, whether a "private language" might be logically possible, a disengaged system that because of its self-referentiality would not enclose the propositional world. Several times, Wittgenstein revisits those metaphors of spatiality and interiority that characterize his friend Trakl's almost egoless diction:

> 6.522    There is indeed the inexpressible. This shows itself; it is the mystical. [...]

6.54    My propositions are elucidatory in this way: he who understands me finally recognizes them as senseless, when he climbs out through them, on them, over them. [...]

7    Whereof one cannot speak, thereof one must be silent.

Reading Trakl's first book, in 1915, Rainer Maria Rilke hears the mystery of this provocative silence echo in the mirror-space of regressive interiority in the poems:

Trakl's experience occurs like mirror images and fills its entire space, which, like the space in the mirror, cannot be entered.

"Who," Rilke wonders, "must he have been?"

\*

In the last several decades, several worthwhile English-language translations of Trakl's poems have appeared, each with its own implied answer to versions of Rilke's question. I have learned much from those translations, as well as from English- and German-language criticism of the work. Nevertheless, I wanted to try to translate a new selection of the poems, for several reasons.

First, over time I've come to hear a unique tone of voice informing the sequence of perceptions in these poems, a tone I wanted to try to convey. Elegant and specific, the tone accumulates strength as the young poet enlarges his scope, eventually moving toward a complex perspective: a fierce intensity of perception and yet an almost Buddhist dispassion. Its language evolves, becoming more declarative and concise, a Romanticism turned raw and wry. And it can be grimly witty, self-knowing in its hauteur. Despite the gloom and the repetitive lament in tone, the style of the voice is mellow, elegant, even droll in its burnished factuality. Trakl's repetitions matter (they are not compulsions but patterned choices); his factuality dares; his neologisms are dense, but they are organized in a grammar of radical simplicity. Trakl seldom exaggerates; he does not whine; he does not turn away.

I wanted to try to register, in English, that droll, ascetic tone. I tend not to hear the *cri de coeur* of a young Expressionist victim (as he's sometimes represented, and as his life story sometimes seems to invite). Instead, I see the odd olive-and-ochre factuality of his self-portrait, the craft of an accomplished artist as he follows through on his aesthetic commitments, even in the face of horrible circumstances. Trakl's tone in the later poems points toward something ineffable while acknowledging that our indications do not name it or invent it, whatever that meaning is. Language may embody it but cannot say it. Mysteriously, words may sometimes form images or propositions about it; the embodied mystery stands figuratively "outside" ("before" or "on the way to" language). In Trakl's stark ungodly poems, what usually seems sensible to contemporary readers, the lyric of experience, comes to seem arbitrary, presumptuous. His lyricism is lean and acute: pointing lucidly toward what both is and is not there, firm in its stillness. In his silences I hear confidence, not victimized muteness, and I see clean, conscious craftsmanship in his sentences, lines, and patterns of repetition.

These are oblique, even paradoxical, assumptions for a poet to make: to insist on the powers of silence, incompletion, and pauses; to insist that language conceals to the degree that it reveals, that necessary images distort and disappoint. And yet the ineffable speaks through us. In his late lecture/essay on Trakl ("Language in the Poem," 1951/1959), Martin Heidegger identifies this poetry not by its location but by its momentum and its traces, sites "on the way to language." This aesthetic aims to make possible "a dialogue between thinking and poetry," "to call forth the nature of language, so that mortals may learn again to live within language."

Second, in addition to this question of tone, I have wanted to translate Trakl's poems for reasons involving form, closely related to those earlier questions of tone. After late 1911 and his abandonment of rhymed quatrains, Trakl's diction sounds not so nominative and Teutonically in-stressed as we tend to think. In this set of translations, I have wanted musically to try to capture some of the elegance of his formal choices (an unadorned elegance that shines brightly even as the speaker disappears and reappears) and with it the genuine wit and authority in that voice. Too much unrelieved grief and complaint can seem static, but the voice I hear is seldom stalled in lyrical lament. The forms of his expression are not stalled, or stunned, or repetitive in trauma; in fact, what draws me to these poems is often a Stoic, brave use of form. There is a wit at work, especially in the motion-of-perception connecting lines in Trakl's individual images and in their sequenced argument-by-image. In this vein, Trakl's line breaks carry weight by means of their postponements, their hauntedness, which is often the result of an active, strategic deferral of grammatical meaning, in the sentence or in the line (a function of German syntax that Trakl exploits masterfully). He's read as a deeply internalized writer, recording states of the soul, but I find that things are constantly changing and moving through these poems, often just having passed away or just about to appear: people or objects make their sounds, then keep vibrantly still. His hushes and pauses have volition and momentum. Trakl's repeated verb "schweigen" is "to be [to keep] silent": to *perform the act of* keeping still, actively and forcefully. "Whereof one cannot speak" nevertheless manifests itself. By contrast, Rilke's Orpheus succeeds by gorgeously failing, his lopped head singing even as it floats down the river. I revere Rilke, but the angel of his ambition (as Rilke himself warns) is a "terrible" power of presence; Trakl's angel consoles, to the degree that consolation is possible, and then withdraws.

The third reason I wanted to translate a selection of Trakl's poems has to do with principles of selection and editing, and with a sense of our expectations as English-language readers.

Our narrative of Trakl's life and work tends to emphasize the end of his life, both biographically (the traumatic events on the Eastern Front in WWI, the suicide of the glamorous, suffering young poet) and textually (the apparently sudden consolidation of his poetic strengths around his final poems). These facts are accurate, but we're left wondering how the pieces fit together, how the life and the art inform each other. The poems from "The Heart" to "Grodek" are a continuous sequence of all his last poems (edited and published posthumously by Ficker and given in full in most German editions). This selection renders those last poems as a sequence but leads up to them with representative poems from Trakl's earlier work, to suggest the continuity of his development: from the melancholy of his earliest poems through the "gentle madness" of the middle period, to the fierce objectivity of the end. The last series seem to me to register not so much a rupture under the stress of experience as a rapid consolidation of several motions in long trajectory. The disillusionment of the final poems springs, ironically, from a powerful prior idealism. One hears versions of that idealism, through various modes, in the poems about childhood, in the *alter ego* poems, in the Sister poems, even in the last sequence.

I hope that a continuous edition of a selected poems in a fresh translation can show some of the ruptures *and* some of the continuities of Trakl's art, under the circumstantial and psychological pressures of his life: to help us measure how craft can shape the facts of a life, inventing the life it describes, or "expressing" the experience or the feel of a consciousness, or (as in the last poems) raging against the waste of war. These questions are constantly revisited, in our poetics and in our society. In addition to the Stoic tone, *and* the elegant and musical tact of his forms, I wanted to translate his poems with an eye toward the continuity of his work: I read him as an artist of craft and vitality and fierce moral strength.

*Stephen Tapscott*

# GEORG TRAKL: POEMS

# Cemetery, St. Peter's Church

All around, the solitude of cliffs.
Pale flowers of the dead shiver
on the graves, which mourn in the dark —
and yet this mourning holds no grief.

The sky smiles quietly down
into this garden, closed in its dream,
which the silent pilgrims tend.
A cross stands watch on every grave:

the chapel rises like an appeal
before an icon of eternal grace.
Some light shines down the colonnade,
mute entreaty for these poor souls —

while through the night the trees keep blooming:
so that death's face may hide itself
in the tremulous fullness of that beauty
and make the dead dream deeper.

# Music in Mirabell

A fountain sings. The clouds hang
white and delicate in the clear blue sky.
With measured steps, people walk quietly
through the old garden, at evening.

The ancestral marble has turned to grey.
A bird's flight cruises through the distance.
A faun with dead eyes watches
for shadows that glide through the dusk.

From the old tree, one leaf detaches
and wheels through an open window.
In the room, the brightness of a fire glows
and sketches eerie specters.

A pale stranger steps into the house.
A dog lopes down the leaf-littered paths;
a girl extinguishes a lamp; the ear
listens for sonatas playing.

# Rondel

The gold of day has passed away.
The browns and blues of the evening.
The shepherds' gentle pipes are ending
the browns and blues of the evening.
The gold of day has passed away.

# De Profundis (I)

Perfectly night, the chamber of the dead
as my father sleeps, and I stand guard.

The dead man: his hard face, white,
flickers in the candlelight.

Flowers ply their sweetness. One fly hums.
My heart listens, speechless and numb.

The wind knocks softly at the door;
brightly it creaks; it leans ajar.

Beyond, a field of wheat is rustling.
Sunlight crackles in the sky's pavilion.

Bush and tree droop full with fruit;
moths and birds swoop through the room.

In the fields the workers thresh
through the depth of noontime hush.

I let the cross drop on the dead; soundless
through the grass, my footsteps dissolve.

# Sunny Afternoon

In the deep blue, a bough gently rocks me.
In the crazy leaf-babble of the fall
butterflies flutter, tipsy and wild.
Ax-strokes echo in the lea.

I bite red berries with my mouth;
light and shadow waver in the leaves.
Hours-long, the golden pollen sifts
crackling on the brownish ground.

A thrush is laughing from out of the bush,
and crazy and loud the autumn babble
of the leaves engulfs me.
Shining and plump, the fruits break loose.

## Trumpets

Under polled willows, where sun-tanned children play
and leaves drift, trumpets sound. A graveyard-shudder.
Scarlet flags plunge through the sorrow of the maples:
horsemen along the rye-fields, empty granaries.

Or: shepherds sing in the night, and deer step
into the ring of their fire, the ancient sadness of the woods.
Dancers throw themselves up a black parapet:
scarlet flags, laughter, madness, trumpets.

# The Rats

In the courtyard palely the autumn moon shines.
Phantom shadows drop from the eaves.
A silence dwells in the empty windows
where softly the rats emerge

and scuttle, squeaking, back and forth;
through the grayish haze that whuffs
behind them from the shed
a spectral moonlight shudders,

and they clatter greedily as if insane
and overrun the house and barns
that are full of fruits and grain.
Icy winds whimper in the dark.

# Rosary Songs

*To Sister*

Where you are, there autumn and evening are,
a blue deer that makes its sound among the trees,
solitary pond at evening.

Softly the flight of a bird makes its sound,
the sorrow across your eye's curved brow.
Your slight smile makes its sound.

God has wrenched the lids of your eyes.
Good-Friday's-child, at night the stars
seek out the curve of your forehead.


*The Nearness of Death*

O the evening, that enters the dark villages of childhood.
The pond beneath the willow
fills with sorrow's toxic sighs.

O the woods, which gently make brown eyes close,
as the crimson of those enraptured days
pours from the solitary's bony hands.

O the nearness of death. Let us pray.
Tonight, across negligent cushions may lovers,
gilded by incense, loosen their delicate limbs.

*Amen*

Some decayed thing, slipping through the ramshackle room:
shadows on yellow tapestries; across dark mirrors, bending,
the ivory sorrow of our hands reaches out.

Brown beads trickle through withered fingers.
In the stillness
the poppy-blue eyes of an angel open.

The evening, too, is blue:
the hour of our undoing, the shadow of Azraël,
that darkens a little bronze garden.

# Evening Song

At evening, when we walk the dark paths,
our own pale forms appear before us.

When we feel thirsty,
we drink white water from the pond,
sweetness of our poignant childhood.

Dead-tired, we rest beneath the elderberry;
we watch the grey gulls.

Spring clouds loom over the dark city,
making the higher time — the time of the monks — go quiet.

As I took your slender hand,
gently you opened your wide eyes.
That was long ago.

And yet, when dark harmonies haunt the soul, then
you appear, Whiteness, in your friend's autumn-landscape.

# Helian

In the solitary hours of the soul,
it's lovely to walk out in the sun
along the summer's yellow walls.
Softly your footsteps ring in the grass; still, as always,
in the grayish marble the son of Pan is sleeping.

In the evening on the terrace, we drank too much brown wine.
A peach glows rosy in the foliage.
Calm sonata, happy laughter.

It's lovely, the quiet of the night.
On a dark plain
we meet shepherds and white stars.

When autumn has come,
a solemn clarity appears in the grove.
Gentle, we drift beside red walls,
our wide eyes following the flight of birds.
At evening white water settles in urns.

The sky rejoices in the leafless branches.
In clean hands, a farmer carries bread and wine,
and peacefully in the sunny room, fruits ripen.

How solemn it seems, the face of the dead man we loved:
a righteous sight the soul enjoys.

The silence of this neglected garden is strong:
as the novice crowns his forehead with brown leaves,
his breathing drinks in icy gold.

The hands stroke the age of the bluish waters,
or, on a cold night, the Sisters' white cheeks.

It's calm and it's harmonious, to walk through friendly spaces
where solitude is, the rustling of a maple —
where, maybe, a thrush still sings.

Lovely the man appearing in the darkness,
astonished as he moves his arms, his legs,
the eyes rolling quietly in their crimson sockets.

At Vespers the stranger wanders lost through November's wastes,
under brittle branches, along the leper-white walls
where once the holy Brother used to walk,
immersed in the soft string-music of his madness.

How lonely the evening wind subsides.
Dying, the head sinks down, in the dark of the olive tree.

It's unsettling, the waning of a generation.
In this hour the watcher's eyes fill
with the gold of his stars.

At evening the carillon fades, going mute.
The black walls on the city square crumble.
A dead soldier calls out for prayer.

A pale angel,
the son, walks into his father's empty house.

The Sisters are gone — far off, to the white Elders;
by night the sleeper would find them, along the hallway colonnade,
come back from their sad pilgrimages.

Their hair is so stiff, with filth and with worms,
as he stands on his silver feet,
and the lost step forth from the naked rooms.

O you psalms in fiery midnight-rains:
as slaves flailed the gentle eyes with nettles,
the childlike fruits of the elderberry
bend amazed above an empty grave.

Yellowed moons roll softly
over the young man's feverish bed-linen
before it turns to the silence of winter.

A noble destiny broods its way down the Kidron Valley,
where the cedar, tender creature,
unfurls beneath the father's blue brows.
Across the meadow, by night, a shepherd leads his flock
— or else there are cries, in sleep,
when a bronze angel confronts some human in the grove;
the flesh of a saint melts on the glowing grill.

Scarlet vines wind over the clay huts,
ringing sheaves of yellow wheat,
murmur of bees, the flight of a crane.
At evening the resurrected meet, on cliff-rock paths.

In the black waters, lepers are reflected
— or else they open their filth-spattered robes
and cry out to the balsam-wind that drifts from the rosy hill.

Slender girls grope their way down the alley-ways of night,
toward — maybe — the passionate shepherds.
Saturdays: gentle singing in the huts.

Let the song remember, too, that boy,
his madness and white brows, his passing-on:
the one who is decomposing, bluishly opening his eyes.
How sad it is, this rendezvous.

Stairwells of madness in black rooms,
shadows of grown-ups under the open door:
there Helian's soul regards itself in the rosy mirror,
and snow and leprosy drop from his brow.

Along the walls the stars have been extinguished,
and the light's white forms.

Buried bones rise up from the carpet:
the silence of dilapidated crosses on the hill,
the sweetness of incense in the night's crimson wind.

You, shattered eyes in black mouths:
as the grandchild, in his gentle delirium,
in solitude ponders the darker ending,
the silent god lowers his blue eyelids over him.

## To the Young Elis

Elis, when the thrush cries in the black woods,
that's when you fall.
Your lips drink the coolness of the blue rock-spring.

Let go, as your forehead softly bleeds
ancient legends
and the dark augury of the flight of birds.

And yet you pass with soft steps into the night
that hangs full of crimson grapes,
and you move your arms, even more finely, through the blue air.

Where your moonlike eyes are,
there a thorn-bush sounds.
How long it is, O Elis, since you have passed away.

Your body is a hyacinth
a monk with waxen fingers submerges.
Our silence is a black cave

from which, sometimes, a gentle animal comes out,
lowering its heavy eyelids slowly.
Onto your temples a black dew drops,

last gold of ruined stars.

# Horror

I watched myself walk through deserted rooms.
— The stars danced demented on their blue foundations.
Dogs were howling across the fields,
and the wind gnawed wild in the tree-tops.

Then abruptly: silence! A muffled fever
forced poison flowers to bloom from my mouth:
from the stems, as from a wound, a pale dew dropped,
shimmering, and dropped, and dropped like blood.

Out of the mendacious void of a mirror,
out of horror and darkness, slowly
as though casually, a face rose: Cain.

Softly the velvet curtains rustled:
through the window the moon glanced into the void,
and I was alone with my assassin.

# Elis

1.
Perfect, the stillness of this golden day.
Under ancient oaks
you appear, Elis: serene, with open eyes.

Their blueness recalls the slumber of lovers.
On your mouth
their rosy sighs fell silent.

At evening the fisherman drew in his heavy nets.
A good shepherd
guides his flock on the verge of the forest.
How righteous, Elis, are all your days!

It goes down so slowly,
the olive's blue stillness along the barren wall;
the dark song of an old man dies away.

A golden boat,
your heart, Elis, rocks in the solitary sky.

2.
A soft carillon rings in Elis' breast
at evening,
as his head sinks back in the black pillow.

A wild blue beast
bleeds softly in the brambles.

There a brown tree stands, secluded,
its blue fruits dropped away.

Signs and stars
gently go under, in the evening-pond.

Behind the hill, winter has arrived.

Blue doves
sip nightly at the icy sweat
that slips down Elis' crystal forehead.

Constantly it sounds
along the black walls, God's lonely wind.

# Landscape

September evening: the dark calls of the shepherds ring sadly
through the twilit little town. Fire spritzes in the forge.
A black horse rears back, strong. The hyacinth-curls of a girl's hair
tangle in the heat of its crimson nostrils.
Faintly at the edge of the woods, the cry of the doe turns into a
    stare,
and autumn's yellow flowers
bend mute above the blue countenance of the pond.
A tree is consumed, in red flame. Bats flutter up with dark faces.

# Hush

Over the woods palely it shines,
the moon, that makes us dream.
The meadow by the dark pond
soundlessly weeps into the night.

A heart extinguishes, and softly
the mists swirl and rise:
hush.  hush.

# Night Song

Come fetch me, pain! My wound brightens.
I am indifferent to this torment.
Out of these wounds something is growing,
look: a star in the night, beyond our knowing.
Come fetch me, Death. I am perfected.

# De Profundis (II)

There is a field of stubble, where a black rain falls.
There is a brown tree that stands alone.
There is a whispering wind that circles the empty sheds.
How sad this evening is.

Beyond the settlement
a gentle orphan-girl gleans the meager grain.
Her eyes grow wide, round and gold in the dusk,
and her womb awaits the heavenly bridegroom.

On their way home
shepherds found the sweet dead body
decaying in the thornbush.

I am a shadow far from the dark towns.
The silence of God:
I drank it from the spring in the grove.

Cold metal oozes from my forehead.
Spiders explore my heart.
There is a light that dies in my mouth.

At night I found myself in a meadow
thick with filth and the dust of stars.
In the hazelbush
crystal angels were ringing, again.

# December

At evening jongleurs parade through the woods
with fabulous carriages, little horses. In the clouds
a golden treasure-chest appears, shut tight.
Villages stand out as if painted on the white plateau.

Dark and cold, the wind swings its shield and cudgels;
a raven trails after the sullen company.
A ray of light falls from the sky to the bloody gutters,
and gently a funeral surges toward the churchyard.

The shepherds' huts dwindle in the grey, nearby;
a gleam as of old jewels sparkles on the pond;
farmers sit down to a flagon of wine.

Shyly, a boy sidles up to a girl.
Look: there's the sexton in the sacristy,
and red tools, beautiful and cryptic.

# The Law

The cottages of childhood are, in autumn,
ruined hamlets: dark shapes,
mothers singing in the evening wind:
at the windows, *Angelus* and folded hands.

Dead birth: on the green ground
the secrecy of bluish flowers, their stillness.
Madness opens its scarlet mouth,
*dies irae*, the grave, and stillness.

Gropings through green thorns;
in sleep: bloody sputum, hunger, and laughter;
fire in the village, waking in the wild;
terror and tossing in the gurgling skiff.

Or, leaning on the wooden stairway
again, the strange woman of white shadows.
The poor sinner yearning toward the blue sky
abandons his foulness to the lilies and the rats.

## Sister's Garden

Soon it will be cool, soon it will be late,
autumn has already come
to Sister's garden, quiet and mild:
her footstep has become white.
The call of a blackbird drifts and fades:
autumn has already come
to Sister's garden, quiet and mild:
an angel has become.

## Wind, white voice...

Wind, white voice, that whispers at the drunken forehead;
dissolving path. Long evening-bells sank into the slime of the
    ponds
where the golden flowers of autumn droop. There, with their
    demented faces,
the bats flicker.

Home! Sunset-pink mountains! Peace! Purity!
The caw of the buzzards! Lonely, the heavens darken;
the white head sinks powerfully down at the edge of the woods.
Night climbs out of the dark ravine.

Around the sleeper, flourishing childish sunflowers flutter.

## To Novalis

The holy stranger rests in dark earth.
God received the dirge from his soft modest mouth
as he sank back, in his bloom-time.
One blue flower
sustains his song, in pain's nocturnal house.

# With Young Wine

The sun is setting crimson.
The swallow's long since flown.
Under the arches of the evening
the young wine makes its round.
Child: your wild laughter.

Grief, in which the world turns.
Stilly, the moment remains
when, under the wooden arches of evening
the young wine makes its round.
Child: your wild laughter.

A flicker of starlight drifts at the window:
the black night is drawn along,
as in the shadow of the dark arches
the young wine makes its round.
Child: your wild laughter.

# Night-Cries

over the crumpled foreheads night has opened
with lovely stars
over the faces petrified with pain
a wild beast gnaws the affectionate heart
an angel of fire
stumbles with broken torso through the rocky field
a buzzard rises    flapping
grief in an unending wail
commingles fire    earth    blue source

## Plea

*to Lucifer*


Send your flames into the soul, it suffers so,
sighing trapped in black midnight
on the springtime hill: so the gentle lamb,
the one who endures the deepest pain, offers itself:
O love that like a ball of light
rises in the heart and endures such a gentleness
that this earthen vessel shatters.

# Psalm

Stillness: as if the blind sank down by an autumn wall,
listening, with fragile brows, to the river of crows;
autumn's gold stillness, the father's face in the flickering sun;
at evening the old village settles back, in the peace of the brown
    oaks;
the red hammering of the smith, a pounding heart.
Stillness: in her slow hands she holds her temples, like a
    hyacinth, the girl
under the fluttering sunflowers. Fear and the silence
of dimming eyes fill the twilit room, the angry pacing
of the old woman, the scarlet mouth's trajectory, slowly
    dissolving in the dark.

An evening going mute, in wine. From the lowest rafters
a night-moth dropped, a nymph interred in bluish sleep.

In the courtyard a boy slaughters a lamb; the sweet scent of the
    blood
floats in a cloud around his brow, the dark cool of the fountain.
The sadness of the dying asters mourns into the night, gold
    voices in the wind.
When night comes you watch me with moldering eyes,
with your cheeks, in blue silence, decayed into dust.
As gently as a brushfire burning down, the dark hamlet goes
    silent in its field:
as if the cross came down from Calvary's blue hill,
as if the silent earth disgorged its dead.

# Age

They glow ethereally, the wild
roses on the garden-trellis:
O — silent soul!

The crystal sun grazes through
the cool vine-leaves:
O — holy purity!

With courteous hands an old man offers
ripened fruit.
O — glimpse of love!

# The Sunflowers

You gold sunflowers
bowing inwardly toward dying,
you humble sisters:
in a stillness like this
it ended, Helian's year
of mountainous coolness.

Where his intoxicated face
pales with kisses,
among such golden
flowers of dejection,
speechless the darkness
that defines the soul.

# The West

1.
Moon, as if a dead thing
stepped out of a blue cave;
from among the flowers, many
fall across the rocky path.
Something infirm cries, silver
by the evening pond.
In a black rowboat
lovers died, crossing over.

Or as if footsteps rang,
those of Elis, through the grove
like a hyacinth,
fading then under the oaks.
O the figure of that boy,
formed of crystal tears,
night-shadows.
Jags of lightning brighten his temples,
ever-cool,
when a springtime storm
rumbles over the green hill.

2.
The green woods are so quiet
in our homeland,
the crystal wave
expiring along the crumbled wall,
and we have wept in our sleep:
along the thorny hedge
singers through the summer evening
wander with hesitant steps,
in the holy peace

of the vineyards, distantly radiant:
shadows now in the cool womb
of the night, mournful eagles.
So, softly, a moonbeam heals
sorrow's crimson emblems.

3.
You great cities
built in stone
on the plain!
So, mutely,
the man without a home,
his brow dark, follows the wind,
the naked trees on the hill.
You rivers gleaming like dusk in the distance:
awful the evening's red
that terrifies
among the storm-clouds.
You dying tribes!
A pale wave
breaking on the night's beach,
falling stars.

## In Snow

To concentrate on the truth —
to suffer.
In the end an inspiration —
toward dying.
Winter night,
you — chaste nun!

## [Fragment 7]

The homeless man turns
back to the mossy woods

# Childhood

The elderberry is heavy with fruit; childhood lived quietly
in a blue cave. Over the bygone path
where the wild grass whistles brown now,
the quiet boughs brood: a rustling of leaves,

like blue water as it sounds along a cliff.
Gentle, the thrush's lament. A shepherd
wordlessly follows the sun as it rolls down autumn's hill.

One blue moment is still more spirit.
From the verge of the woods a shy deer emerges; peacefully
old bells and dark villages rest in the earth.

More devoutly now, you know the import of dark years,
coolness and autumn in lonely rooms.
Brilliant footfalls ring in the holy blue.

An open window rattles softly. The sight
of a ruined graveyard on the hill brings tears to your eyes,
memories of legends repeated. Still, at times, the soul brightens
when it thinks of joyous people, dark-gold days in the spring.

# Sebastian in Dream

1.
Mother carried the little child in the white moonlight,
in the nut-tree's shadow, the old elder-tree;
drunk on poppy-juice, the mourning of the thrush;
and silently
with pity a bearded face leaned over her,

softly, in the darkness of the window. Old household things,
ancestral things,
lay in rubble; love, and autumn's revery.

And so that day of the year was dark, that sad childhood,
as the boy went down to the cool waters softly, to the silvery fish,
a respite, and a face:
as he threw himself stonily down toward the pounding stallions,
in the grey of night, his star rose over him:

or when he walked holding his mother's icy hand,
at evening, through the autumn graveyard of St. Peter's Church,
a frail corpse lay quiet in the dark of its chamber
and spread its cold eyelids over him.

But he was a little bird in the naked branches:
the bell reached out through the November dusk,
the father's silence, where he walked down the twilit twisting
stairs, in sleep.

2.
Soul's peace. Lonely winter evening,
the dark forms of shepherds by the old pond,
the infant in the straw hut. O how softly
his face sank back, in black fever.
Holy night.

Or when he walked holding his father's firm hand
up the dark Mount of Calvary
and in the twilit clefts of the rocks
the blue shape of humankind would pass through his tales,
the blood flowing crimson from the wound below the heart.
O how softly the cross rose in the dark soul.

Love: as the snow was melting in the black corners,
a blue breeze tangling happy through the old elderberry,
in the shade-vault of the nut-tree,
and softly his rose-colored angel appeared to the boy.

Joy: as an evening sonata rang through the cool rooms,
on a brown ceiling-beam
a blue moth crept from its silver cocoon.

O the nearness of death. From the stony wall
a yellow head bent down, the child keeping silent,
that March, as the moon decayed.

3.

Rose-colored bell of Easter in the vault of the night
and the silver voices of the stars:
so a dark madness dropped in shivers on the sleeper's brow.

O how quiet, to walk by the blue river
thinking about forgotten things, as, from the green branches,
the thrush warbled something strange into the sunset.

Or as he walked, holding the old man's bony hand
at evening, along the city's crumbled walls,
and someone carried a little pink child, wrapped in his black cloak:
then, in the shade of the nut-tree, the spirit of evil appeared.

Groping steps down the summer's green stairway. O how softly
the garden decayed in the bronze stillness of autumn.
The scent and the sadness of the old elder-tree,
as the silver voice of the angel faded in Sebastian's shadow.

# On the Moor

Vagrant in the black wind: softly the reed-stem murmurs
in the stillness of the moor. Along grey sky
a line of wild birds passes,
oblique, over dark water.

Commotion. In a ruined cottage
decay slaps its black wings, rising.
Twisted birches sigh in the wind.

Evening in an empty inn. The placid sadness
of grazing herds enwraps the long way home.
Night's epiphany: toads bubble up from the silver waters.

# Evening in Lans

Walks through dusky summer,
past sheaves of goldening wheat. Under the whitewashed arches
where in and out swallows flew, we drank a fiery wine.

Lovely: O melancholy, and crimson laughter.
Evening and the dark scent of greens
cool our glowing brows with shivers.

Silver waters flow down the forest stairs,
the night, and — speechless — a forgotten life.
Friend: the leaf-covered bridges into the village.

# Song of Kaspar Hauser

He truly loved the sun as it climbed down the hill going crimson,
paths through the forest, the blackbird as it sang,
the gladness of the green world.

Self-possessed where he lived, in the shadow of the tree,
and his aspect was pure.
God spoke a gentle flame into his heart:
O human.

The city felt his footsteps softly in the evening.
His mouth's dark claim was
*I want to be a Horseman.*

But scrub-brush and beast pursued him,
through neighborhoods and twilit-gardens where the
    pallid people lived.
And his killer tracked him down.

Spring and summer and lovely the autumn
of the righteous, his gentle footsteps
down past the dreamers' darkened rooms.
At night he stayed alone with his star,

saw the snow as it fell through naked branches
and, down the corridor of dusk, the assassin's shadow.

Silver it sank, the head of the one who had never been born.

## Surrender to the Night

Holy cloistered sister! close me in your dark,
your cool blue highlands.
Bleeding, the dark dew drains;
the cross juts steep against the sparks of stars.

Crimson the mouth — and the lies — open,
coolly, in a ruined room.
But laughter still sparkles, golden play,
a bell's last exhalations.

Moon-clouds! Wild fruit at evening
drops darkly from the tree.
And space turns to a grave,
and this pilgrimage on earth, to dream.

## At Night

The blueness of my eyes dissolves into this night,
the red gold of my heart. How quietly the lamp burns!
Your blue cloak wrapped the one who is sinking low:
your red mouth set its seal on your friend's encroaching dark.

# A Winter Evening
*first version*


As the snow falls on the window,
the evening-bell rings in the distance.
The table is set, ready for many,
and the house is well-provisioned.

Sometimes a traveler comes up
the dark paths, to the door.
Graciously, love's tender power
heals his injuries.

O — the sheer human suffering!
The man struck mute by wrestling angels,
mastered by divine pain: quietly
he longs for the bread and wine of God.

# A Winter Evening

*second version*

As the snow falls on the window,
the evening-bell rings in the distance.
The table is set, ready for many,
and the house is well-provisioned.

Sometimes a traveler comes up
the dark paths, to the door.
The tree of magnanimity blooms golden,
out of the earth's fresh sap.

Traveler, step gently within;
suffering has turned the lintel to stone.
There, glowing pure and bright
on the table: bread and wine.

# Birth

Mountain-range: blackness, silence, and snow.
The hunt hikes down, flushed, from the forest.
O the mossy stares of the prey.

The mother's stillness: under black firs
sleeping hands open,
as the cold moon rises in decay.

O the birth of the human. At night, in a rush,
blue water pours over the stony riverbed.
The fallen angel, sighing, glimpses his likeness.

Something pale wakens in the musty room.
Two moons
gleam in the eyes of the stony old woman.

*Aeie!* Wails of birth-pangs. With black wing
the night touches the infant's brow:
snow, dropping softly from a crimson cloud.

## To Those Who Have Gone Mute

O the madness of the grand city, when at evening
gnarled trees stand stiff along the black wall.
From behind a silver mask, the spirit of evil watches:
light, with a magnetic scourge, drives off the stony night.
O the drowned tolling of the evening bells.

Whore who births a dead child, with icy contractions.
Raging, God's wrath flogs the brow of someone possessed.
Crimson plague, hunger, that shatters green eyes.
O the horrible laughter of gold.

But a quieter humankind bleeds in silence, in a dark cave —
forming, in fierce metals, the head that redeems.

# The Damned

1.
It's evening. The old women walk to the fountain.
In the dark of the chestnut trees, something red laughs.
The smell of bread drifts from a shop,
and sunflowers droop over the fence.

A tavern echoes by the river, mild and faint.
A guitar hums; a jingling of coin.
A halo distinguishes that little girl,
gentle and pale, who waits beside the glass door.

O blue gleam she wakens in the window-pane,
framed by briars, black and enchanted.
A hunchbacked clerk laughs as if deranged
into the water, setting off a wild commotion.

2.
At evening, the plague hems up her blue garment,
and a sinister guest gently closes the door.
The maple's dark burden fades at the window;
a boy rests his forehead in her hand.

Often her eyelids, heavy and sore, sink down.
The child's hands riffle through her hair,
and his tears surge hot and clear
into the dark hollow sockets of her eyes.

A nest of scarlet snakes writhes
sluggishly up from her stirring lap.
Her arms let a dead one drop;
it stitches an edge around the carpet's grief.

3.
A carillon rings into the brown little garden.
Into the dark of the chestnuts something blue floats,
the sweet cloak of an alien woman.
A scent of mignonette, and a glowing sense

of malice. The damp forehead, chilly and pale,
bows down toward the filth where the rats scratch,
bathed gently by the scarlet gleam of stars.
In the garden apples drop, musty and soft.

The night is black. Eerily the foehn-wind billows
the boy's white nightshirt as he walks,
and delicately into his mouth the hand
of the dead woman reaches. Sonia smiles, soft and lovely.

# Transfiguration

When evening comes,
softly, a blue face departs from you.
A little bird sings in the tamarind tree.

A gentle monk
folds the dead hands together.
An angel appears, to visit Mary.

A nocturnal wreath
of violets, wheat, and crimson grapes
— is the year of the man who watches.

At your feet
the graves of the dead open,
as you hold your forehead in your silver hands.

Quietly the autumn moon
dwells on your mouth,
drunk on the poppy-juice of dark song:

blue flower
that softly sounds among the yellowed rocks.

# To One Who Died Young

O, the black angel that stepped out mildly from inside the tree
when we were playmates, in the evening
at the edge of the blue-colored fountain.
Our footfalls were calm, eyes round in the brown cool of autumn.
O, the crimson sweetness of the stars.

But he came down the stone stairs of the Mönchsberg,
a blue smile on his face, and strangely wrapped in his chrysalis-shell,
in his quieter childhood: and he died.
And the friendly silver face remained there, in the garden,
overhearing the leaf, the ancient stones.

Soul sang death, the green decay of the flesh:
it was the rustle of the forest, the cry
of dismay from the breast of the deer.
Always, the blue evening-bells rang from the twilit towers.

The time arrived when he saw the shadows in the crimson sun,
shadows of rot in the naked branches.
At evening, when the blackbird sang by the dusky wall,
the ghost of the one who had died young appeared, quiet, in the
     room.

O the blood that flows from the moaning throat,
blue flower: O the fiery tear

shed in the night.
Gold cloud, and time.  In your solitary chamber,
more often now you invite the dead to be your guest.
You go for long walks, talking easily together, under the elms by the
     green river.

# Karl Kraus

Pale high-priest of truthfulness,
crystal voice the icy breath of God inhabits,
indignant magician:
under your swirling cape, a warrior's armor clangs.

# Passion

As Orpheus silverly strums his lute,
mourning the dead one, in the evening garden,
who are you, who rests under the tall trees?
Some lament rustles through the autumn reeds,
the blue pool
expiring under the greening trees
and following the Sister's shadow.
Dark love
of a wild generation
the day rushes from, on golden wheels.
Silent night.

Under dark firs
two wolves commingled their blood
in a stony embrace; something golden
faded from the cloud above the bridge.
The patience and the noiselessness of childhood.
Once again one sees the delicate lifeless body
at the Triton-fountain,
dozing, his hyacinthine hair.
May his cool head shatter, at last.

For, constantly, a wild blue deer passes
watchful beneath the twilit trees,
along these darker paths,
wakeful and shaken by night-noises.
A gentle madness —
or a dark rapture …echoes,
full of the sound of stringed instruments,
at the cool feet of the woman doing penance
in the stony city.

# Winter Night

It's been snowing. After midnight, drunk on crimson wine, you
leave the dim shelters of humankind, the red fires of their
hearth. O, the darkness!
Black frost. The earth is stiff; the air tastes bitter. Your stars clus-
ter into evil signs.
With stony steps you stamp along the rail-embankment, eyes
wide as a soldier's as he storms a black trench. Onward!
Bitter snow and moon.
A red wolf, which an angel strangles. Pacing, your legs rattle
like blue ice; a smile of grief and haughtiness has turned
your face to stone; your forehead blanches in the bliss of the
frost
or else bends, quietly, over the sleep of the night-watchman
dropping off in his wooden shack.
Frost and smoke. A white shirt of stars burns on your burdened
shoulders, and God's buzzards rip at your heart, hard as
metal.
O, the stony hill. Silent, forgotten, the cold body dissolves into
the silver snow.
It is black, this sleep. For a long time the ear tracks the paths of
the stars, in the ice.
When you awoke, the bells in the village were ringing. The rose-
colored day stepped silver through the eastern gate.

# In Venice

Stillness in the night's room.

The candlesticks flicker silver
before the singing breath
of the solitary man:
mesmerizing rosy clouds.

A black swarm of flies
darkens the stony space,
and the torment of the golden day
clenches stiff the head
of the man who has no home.

Motionless, the sea turns dark.
Star, and a dark journey,
vanished on the canal.
Child, your afflicted smile
followed me softly to sleep.

# The Sun

Each day the yellow sun comes up the hill.
Lovely the woods, the dark animal,
the human: hunter or shepherd.

The fish rises pink in the green pond.
Under the round sky
the fisherman drifts quietly in the blue skiff.

Slowly the grape ripens, and the grain.
As the day slopes stilly away,
something good, and also malign, makes ready.

As night arrives,
quietly the traveler lifts his heavy eyelids.
Sunlight spills through a dark cleft.

# Song of the Caged Blackbird

Dark breath among green branches.
Blue blossoms float around the face
of the solitary, the golden footstep
fading, under the olive-tree.
The night flutters up on a drunken wing.
Humility: it bleeds so softly,
a dew, oozing a drop from the flowering thorn.
Into its luminous arms, compassion
gathers a shattered heart.

# Summer

At evening the cuckoo stops
its crying in the woods.
The wheat bends lower,
the red poppy.

A black storm threatens
over the hill.
The old song of the cricket
fades in the field.

Unmoving, the leaves
of the chestnut.
Along the spiral stairs
your dress rustles.

Quietly the candle glimmers
in the dark room;
a silver hand
extinguishes it.

Wind-quiet, starless night.

# Decline

Over the white pond
the wild birds have already passed.
In the evening, an icy wind blows from our stars.

Over our graves
the shattered forehead of the night bends.
Under oaks we rock in a silver boat.

The white walls of the city keep chiming.
Under arcs of thorn,
O my brother we blind hands advance toward midnight.

# [Aphorism]

In moments of deathlike existence you feel: everyone is worthy
of love.
Awakening, you feel the bitterness of the world; inside it is all
your unresolved guilt, your poem an imperfect atonement.

# In Hellbrunn

Once more, following the blue lament of the evening
along the hill, along the springtime pond —
as if the shades of those long dead hovered there,
shades of high prelates, of noble-women — :
their flowers are already opened, their solemn violets
in the depth of the evening, and the murmur of the blue spring's
crystal wave. So, ghostly, the oak-trees grow
green along the bygone paths of the dead,
the golden cloud above the pond.

# The Heart

The wild heart blanched at the forest —
O dark fear
of death — just as the gold
in a gray cloud died.
November evening.
At the bare gate of the abbatoir
the mob of poor women waited:
into each basket
rancid meat and offal dropped,
abominable stuff.

Evening's blue dove
brought no appeasement.
Dark calls of trumpets
drive through the elms'
moist gold foliage —
a flag in shreds
and smoldering with blood — :
so a man in a wild despair
pays attention there.
O you iron-ore seasons
interred in the sunsct.

Out of the dark vestibule
the golden form
of the Virgo stepped —
ringed by pale moons,
her autumn retinue:
black firs crumpled
in the night-storm,
the cliff-sheer fortress.
O heart,
shimmering out into the snowy cold.

# Sleep

Damn you, dark toxins,
white sleep!
This bizarre garden
of dusk-lit trees —
full of snakes, of night-moths,
spiders, bats.
Stranger! your shadow, lost
in the sunset:
a grim corsair
on misery's salt sea.
White birds flap up on the margin of the night,
over collapsing cities
of steel.

# The Storm

You wild mountains, eagle-
lifted grief.
Gold clouds
smolder over stony wastes.
The pines exhale their patient stillness:
black lambs near a chasm,
how quickly the blueness
turns oddly mute,
soft humming of the bumblebees.
O green flower —
O noiselessness.

Like a dream, in the torrent obscure spirits
startle the heart,
darkness
closing in over the gorges!
White voices
wandering through horrible porticos,
shattered terraces,
the fierce wrath of the father, wails
of the mother,
the boy's gold battle-cries
and the unborn,
sighing, through blind eyes.

O suffering, you flaring glimpse
of the greater spirit!
Already through the black crush
of horses and wagons
a rose-colored shudder of lightning
convulses the echoing spruce.
A magnetic coolness

hovers around this proud head,
the radiant sadness
of an angry god.

Fear, you poison snake,
you blackness: die among the rocks.
There the wild stream
of tears plunges,
storm-merciful,

echoing in rumbling thunders
around the snowy peaks.
Fire
purifies the shattered night.

# The Evening

Dead heroic shapes:
moon, you fill
the silent woods with them —
sickle-moon —
with the gentle caresses
of lovers,
the shades of celebrated eras
around the moldern cliffs:
the moon glows so bluish
against the city,
where, cold and malign,
a corrupt generation lives,
preparing a dark future
for their pale descendants.
You moon-webbed shadows,
fading in the empty crystal
of the mountain lake.

# The Night

You I sing, wild abyss
in the night's storm,
mountains towering up:
you, grey towers
seething with hellish grimaces,
with fiery beasts,
grim ferns, spruces,
crystalline flowers.
Endless torment
for you, to chase after God —
O gentle spirit,
sighing in the waterfall,
in the surging pines.

Golden the fires of the nations
blaze, all around.
Over blackish cliffs
the radiant whirlwind
plunges, deadly-drunk,
the blue upswelling
of the glacier
and the bell in the valley
tolling violently:
flames, curses,
and the dark
contests of lust:
a fossilized head
storms against the sky.

# Misery

You're strong, dark mouth,
from within, configured
out of autumn-clouds,
gold evening silence:
greenish mountain-stream that flickers
through the shadowland
of broken pines:
a village
dies out piously, in brown images.

There black horses leap
across the misty field.
You, soldiers!
Along the hill where the sun rolls dying
the laughing blood plunges —
under oaks,
speechlessly! O the rumbling misery
of the army: a shining helmet
fell clanging from a crimson brow.

The autumn night comes on so coolly:
above the shattered bones of men
she shines, radiant with stars:
the silent nun.

# The Eastern Front

The wild pipe organs of the winter storm
are like a people's grim wrath,
like the crimson surge of battle,
defoliated stars.

With shattered brows, with silver arms,
night reaches out toward the dying soldiers.
In the shadow of the autumn ash-tree
the souls of the slaughtered sigh.

A thorny wilderness winds around the city.
Along bleeding stairwells the moon chases
the terrified women.
Wild wolves have broken through the gate.

# Threnody

Sleep and death, those solemn eagles,
wheel all night around this head.
Humanity's golden image may
be swallowed by the icy wave
of eternity. Against grim reefs
the crimson body grinds to pieces,
and the dark voice cries out
over the sea.
Sister of stormy grief,
look: a tremulous boat
capsizes under stars,
under the expressionless face of the night.

# Grodek

At evening the autumn woods echo
with deadly weapons, the gold plains
and blue lakes the sun rolls
solemnly across. Night wraps
the dying warriors, the wild plaintive cries
from their broken mouths.
Yet stilly in the willow-valley
red clouds gather, where a god of wrath lives:
all the spilt blood, a coolness like the moon's.
The paths flow together, into a black decay.
Under the golden branches of the night and stars,
the shadow of the Sister shimmers through the silent grove
to greet the ghosts of the heroes, the bleeding heads,
and the dark flutes of autumn sound softly through the reeds.
O prouder sorrow! You, bronze altars,
the soul's hot flame is fueled today by a mighty grief:
generations not to be born.

# A Note on the Texts

Although he'd published dozens of poems in periodicals, Georg Trakl saw only one short book appear in print during his life. That book, *Gedichte / Poems*, came out in 1913, thanks largely to his friend and mentor Ludwig von Ficker. Trakl left a manuscript-sketch of a second book, which included poems from his "middle period" in Innsbruck, ca. 1912–13. After Trakl's death in November 1914, Ficker published that second collection as *Sebastian im Traum / Sebastian in Dream*. Trakl left also a small posthumous mountain range of poems, variants, drafts, short prose, and scraps. Like the German high-Romantic poets, he also had a fondness for the aphorism and for the "fragment" as a form, making it difficult at times to determine whether a poem is in-process or is a "finished" fragment. Many of these materials are now stored in the Library and Research Collection in the Traklhaus, his birthplace, in Salzburg. Over several generations, these materials have been published in increasingly fuller editions.

I base these translations on the German texts of Trakl's poems in the comprehensive *Dichtung und Briefe*, edited by Walther Killy and Hans Szklenar, published by Otto Mueller (two volumes, Salzburg, 1969). This collection, a new selection and translation, offers poems and drafts in the order in which Trakl wrote them. (The few exceptions involve the dating of individual drafts or versions; Trakl often worked on several poems at the same time, and so drafts can overlap.) The purpose of this chronological ordering is to emphasize overarching continuities and ruptures in all the poetic work. The collection integrates, into one continuous sequence, poems-in-published-books *and* magazine-pieces *and* unpublished-pieces, to the extent they can be specifically dated.

This selection is weighted toward Trakl's middle and later poems, though in so short a writing career that distinction can seem slim and arbitrary. The "early" poems are works mostly in regular quatrains from before 1911 (their formal regularity embarrassed Trakl later), and we can accurately call the poems of 1913–14 a "late" period. The "middle" as a mode is harder to define, but it includes Trakl's work in poetic *personae*, and poems around the period of his sister's marriage and miscarriage, through 1912–13. This book pays attention to the poems that anticipate, or speak to, important later works. It includes some early formalist poems and experiments, at the start; in the middle, this selection includes middle-poems of Trakl's "masks," both imaginary (beatific Sebastian; young Helian, bewildered by experience) and quasi-historical (Kaspar Hauser; Elis Fröbom, who drowned in a well on his wedding day but was revived decades later uncorrupted), and poems addressed to the Sister (a figure of transcendent purity and pre-linguistic integrity) who appears in the poems frequently from 1912 to the end of Trakl's life. Of course, this collection includes all the poems from Trakl's magnificent final series, from "The Heart" to "Grodek," his last poem.

Making this selection, I have been guided by the principles of choice employed in the poet Marie Luise Kaschnitz's elegant selected-edition of Trakl's poems (*Gedichte*, Bibliothek Kuhrkamp, 1991). Because Trakl died young and unpublished, much of his work was edited posthumously from manuscripts; many poems exist in alternate versions, some rough and some apparently completed. For the most part, like Killy-and-Szklenar, and like Kaschnitz, I trust later revisions to signal Trakl's preference. I think it's fair to conclude that Trakl did intend eventually for one version of each poem to be more or less definitive; I don't think that, like Emily Dickinson, he's choosing/ not choosing when he proliferates alternatives in manuscript. He simply did not live to choose, or to complete the revision of some poems.

Trakl tended to revise toward greater succinctness and intensity of diction. He seldom spoils a poem by revision, but he often does change a poem radically in the process of completing it. The only poem included here in two variations is the "Winterabend" / "A Winter Evening" of 1913; it's included twice because it's famous in two versions. First, Trakl wrote about a draft of the poem in a letter to Karl Kraus and included the draft in the letter. Second, in an essay of 1951 (translated into English as "Language in the Poem," 1959), Martin Heidegger does a pivotal reading of the poem; in that famous essay Heidegger discusses the other version of the poem, one that differs significantly (in the final stanza) from the variant that is often anthologized. Both versions are available and known; both are, in fact, plausible readings — one more immanent than the other. I hope that including both versions might serve to illustrate how Trakl's process of revision can involve broad reconceptualization, even though some stanzas can carry over intact from one variant to the next. Sometimes when he revises for style Trakl finds he needs to recast image and argument, too — and vice versa.

In different variants, Trakl dedicated some of these poems to individual persons. The versions of the poems translated here carry these dedications: "The West" ("for Else Lasker-Schüler, with respect"); "Sebastian in Dream" ("for Adolph Loos"); "Song of Kaspar Hauser" ("for Bessie Loos"); "Song of the Caged Blackbird" ("for Ludwig von Ficker"); "Decline" ("for Karl Borromaeus Heinrich").

# Acknowledgments

For permission to use, on the cover, the image from Trakl's "Self-Portrait" ("Selbstporträt des Dichters Georg Trakl"), and for generous access to materials, my thanks to the Trakl-Forchungs-und Gedenkstätte der Salzburger Kulturvereinigung and its director, Herr Dr. Hans Weichselbaum. (Für die Abdruckgenehmigung des Trakl-Selbstporträts danken wir der Georg-Trakl-Forschungs- und Gedenkstätte in Salzburg.)

For the rights to reprint translations, my thanks to the periodicals in which some of these translations first appeared: *Translation* ("Song of Kaspar Hauser," "Elis," "Sebastian in Dream"); *FIELD* ("December," "De Profundis [I]," "Evening Song").

For support in several dimensions, my personal gratitude
— to the Santa Fe Art Institute and to Diane Karp (Director) and Michelle Childs (PR and Residency Director), for a residency-fellowship, sponsored by the Witter Bynner Foundation, and to the Provost's Fund at MIT;
— to Howard (Skip) Eiland who generously took time from his own magisterial work on Walter Benjamin; to Martha Collins, poet and editor;
— and to Christian Hantschk and Brigitte Vavra in Vienna, whose hospitality over the years has offered both a welcome work environment and a welcome escape from the work. Servus, old friends.